KEY S
Parents'
Science H

Author
Dave Wood

Series Editor
Alwyn Morgan

EDUCATIONAL

Every effort has been made to trace copyright holders and to obtain their permission for the use of copyright material. The authors and publishers will gladly receive information enabling them to rectify any error or omission in subsequent editions.

First published 1998

Letts Educational, Schools and Colleges Division,
9-15 Aldine Street, London W12 8AW
Tel: 0181 740 2270
Fax: 0181 740 2280

© Text – Dave Wood
© Illustrations – Letts Educational

Design by Charles Design Associates
Project Management Rosine Faucompre
Illustration by Maxine Handley

British Library Cataloguing-in-Publication Data.
A CIP record for this book is available from the British Library.

ISBN 1 84085 022 1

Printed in Great Britain by Ashford Colour Press

Letts Educational is the trading name of BPP [Letts Educational] Ltd

CONTENTS

Introduction   2

Science Homework Toolkit   8

Key Stage 2   10

About the Activities   16

   In the Kitchen...   17

   Mealtimes...   20

   In the Bathroom...   22

   In the Garden...   25

   Down the Street...   31

   On your Bike...   35

   In the Park...   36

   Up in the Sky...   38

   At the doctor's...   40

   Relaxing at Home...   42

Glossary   44

The purpose of this guide is to encourage children and parents to realise that science is all around us. Everything that we see or do involves some scientific idea or another.

Science should not be seen as a subject which is only studied at school but as something which is a part of everyday life. Science seeks to explain our everyday existence and the natural events which affect our lives.

All children ask questions about the world around them, such as "How does this work?" or "Why does that happen?" As a parent, you play an important role as your responses to these questions may well lay the foundations for your children's attitudes towards science.

We are not trying to make parents into teachers, but to provide starting points for talking about the scientific world. Parents' scientific knowledge will vary and some of you may feel you are not able to answer your child's

Where did I come from?

questions adequately. This does not matter unless the response is just a bare, "I don't know!" It is much better to follow up with, "Let's try to find out," or "Why don't you ask your teacher tomorrow?"

The starting points in this guide can lead to shared activities and joint investigations at home. It is not intended that children should work alone but simply share their ideas with other members of the family and friends.

The discussion and exchange of ideas is important. Working things through together will help to develop your child's understanding and in turn raise their attainment levels.

Books, including encyclopaedias, are a great source of information. There are plenty of good science books on the market, suitable for a range of ages, which you may find very useful. There are also plenty of good titles to be found in libraries.

If children have difficulty in reading them, then read to them or with them and talk about the ideas.

For those who have access to a computer, there are a number of CD ROMs available which hold a wealth of scientific information.

An important part of 'doing science' is learning to use different sources of information effectively.

REMEMBER...

- Try to find opportunities to talk about scientific ideas with your child and make it as natural as possible.

- If possible try to use your child's questions as starting points. Ask them leading questions, such as "Why do you think only some things float?"

- Talk with the children not at them. Share ideas and encourage them to contribute.

- Try to use open ended questions rather than closed ones. For example, "Where shall we plant it?" rather than "Plant it here." Other useful questions include: "Tell me how…?", "What is happening now…?", "I wonder why…?"

- It is important to try to match the activity and amount of work to the child's ability, age and interest. A little and often is the best way forward.

- Be patient. Give your child time to think and work out their ideas. Don't expect too much too soon.

- Don't get upset or frustrated if your child 'misses the point' or does not finish a task.

- Always encourage and be positive – provide plenty of praise.

- Try to build up confidence by concentrating on your child's successes.

- If boredom or frustration is clearly setting in, then stop. Return to the idea at a later date with a fresh mind and renewed enthusiasm.

- Remember it is perfectly normal to forget things! We all do!

SAFETY

- Science is about investigating and trying things out, but experiments should always be planned in advance.

- Always be on the lookout for possible dangers. Discuss these with your child. Health and safety issues are very important.

- Hot water should be no hotter than 70°C (degrees Celsius) for general experimental work.

- Never experiment with mains electricity.

- Make sure that you know exactly which liquids or powders are being used. Do not leave anything potentially dangerous in young hands.

- Be careful when lifting heavy weights or stretching springs.

- Handling moulds and other microbes can be dangerous.

- Take care that the plants you use are safe and not poisonous or irritant in any way.

- Always be careful how you handle animals.

- All potentially dangerous activities should be closely supervised by an adult.

- **Never** look at the Sun directly or through a magnifying glass, binoculars or a telescope. Instead, you can use binoculars or a telescope to project an image of the Sun onto a piece of white card.

- An HB pencil

- A rubber

- Crayons are useful to colour in charts and to highlight your drawings and diagrams. They can be better than 'felt tips', as these tend to go through paper and often smudge.

- A pencil sharpener

- A 'see through' plastic ruler

- The kitchen offers a range of measuring equipment you may need. Scales to measure mass or weight; and jugs and spoons to measure capacity. Try to make sure that you use 'metric' measures rather than 'imperial'.

mework
.it

- Mugs, beakers and dishes make excellent substitutes for laboratory equipment. They should be transparent and made of plastic, rather than glass, for safety reasons. All containers should be washed thoroughly before returning them to normal use.

- A magnifying glass is useful for looking closely at things.

- You can use lolly sticks for taking samples of materials and stirring. Spoons can be used but they will need to be sterilised in boiling water before being used for food again.

- You will find magnets useful. Fridge magnets or those used in magnetic letters or toys can all be used.

The National Curriculum is organised into four Key Stages.

- Key Stage 1 – age range 5–7.
- Key Stage 2 – age range 7–11.
- Key Stage 3 – age range 11–14.
- Key Stage 4 – age range 14–16.

The science to be taught at Key Stage 2 is described in the *Programme of Study*. This tells teachers what they have to teach. Remember that it covers four school years, so areas of study will be revisited from time to time. Teachers do not simply start at the beginning of the Programme of Study and work through it in order. Each school will have planned to do this in different ways and at different times, using what is known as a scheme of work.

The Programme of Study for science is divided into five main sections:

Sc 0	Common Requirements
Sc 1	Experimental and Investigative Science
Sc 2	Life Processes and Living Things
Sc 3	Materials and their Properties
Sc 4	Physical Processes

The first section (Sc0) details the common requirements which apply to the other four areas of study and lays down what should be provided for pupils in five broad areas:

1 Systematic enquiry
2 Science in everyday life
3 The nature of scientific ideas
4 Communications
5 Health and safety

Each of the other four sections begins by stating that:

"Pupils should be taught..."

This specifies what must be taught, and is divided into several numbered parts. These in turn are divided into smaller sections. Each one is a statement and each is given a letter. Thus it is possible to identify each specific teaching objective in the Programme of Study. For example: Sc2, 2g – "Pupils should be taught the main stages of the human life cycle."

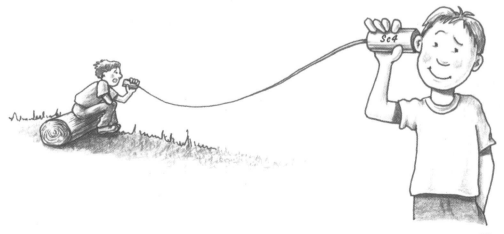

Experimental and Investigative Science aims to teach experimental and investigational methods and is taught in the context of Sc2, 3 and 4 (Life Processes and Living Things, Materials and their Properties and Physical Processes).

The main content of the National Curriculum Programme of Study for Science is as follows:

EXPERIMENTAL AND INVESTIGATIVE SCIENCE

1 Planning experimental work

2 Obtaining evidence

3 Considering evidence

LIFE PROCESSES AND LIVING THINGS

1 Life processes

2 Humans as organisms

3 Green plants as organisms

4 Variation and classification

5 Living things in their environment

MATERIALS AND THEIR PROPERTIES

1 Grouping and classifying materials

2 Changing materials

3 Separating materials

PHYSICAL PROCESSES

1 Electricity

2 Forces and motion

3 Light and sound

4 The Earth and beyond

Towards the end of Key Stage 2, pupils are assessed by National Tests, known as SATs (Standard Assessment Tests), as well as by a Teacher Assessment.

The results are then communicated to parents.

In order to make their assessments teachers use the Level Descriptions in the attainment targets. These describe "*the types and range of performance that pupils working at a particular level should characteristically demonstrate.*"

Using classwork, teachers judge the level which best describes the pupils' performance in each aspect of science.

Pupils at the end of Key Stage 2 should be in the range of Level 2 to Level 5. The higher the level, the better the performance. The expected level for an 'average' 11-year-old is Level 4.

Teacher Assessment Levels are reported in four Attainment Targets:

Sc 1	Experimental and Investigative Science
Sc 2	Life Processes and Living Things
Sc 3	Materials and their Properties
Sc 4	Physical Processes

When reporting to parents at the end of Key Stage 2, schools will give two results for each child. One will be from the test and one from the teacher assessment.

Percentages are also given for pupils in the whole year group attaining each level, as well as the national percentages. These allow parents to compare their school's performance with national averages.

Because science is so much a part of everyday life, many activities that children carry out can be turned to good use in terms of the development of their scientific knowledge.
A few ideas are offered to get you started. You will be able to think of ways to transfer some of them into new situations and come up with many ideas of your own.

The activities are grouped under a range of headings related to the home and neighbourhood.

Good Luck!

I'm sure Science has something to do with this.

GOOD IDEA

In the Kitchen...

The kitchen is a great place for starting science work with materials, particularly relating to **Sc 3 Materials and their Properties**. Many cooking activities involve mixing different materials together in various proportions. The process of cooking itself involves food undergoing permanent changes.

- Choose a favourite recipe for making a cake.

- What ingredients do you use to make the cake and how do they change when you mix them? How do they change again when you bake the cake?

- Try some recipes for other dishes. What changes occur when you cook the food? Try to make a list.

- How many ways can you cook an egg?

- Talk about the difference between bread and toast.

- Look at tins, bottles and jars. What ingredients are in the mixtures? Could they be separated (unmixed)? How would you do this?

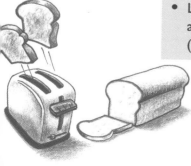

In the Kitchen...

- Talk about substances that dissolve in water, such as jelly, sugar, stock cubes etc. Which substances do not dissolve in water?

- Look for solids, liquids and gases. What are the differences between them? What is their shape? How are they stored or transferred from one place to another?

- Look for 'changes of state' – melting, freezing, boiling, evaporating, condensing. Make a table of your results. What is changing? Why? Are these changes reversible? How could you reverse them?

- Take the temperatures of different items around the kitchen. Make a table of your results.

In the Kitchen...

- Look at kitchen equipment. What does it do? How does it work? Sieves, filters etc. Discuss why different pieces of equipment are suitable for different jobs.

- How do blenders, food processors and mixers work? How is their speed varied? Write a few sentences about the function of different pieces of equipment.

- Washing-up could lead to discussions about cleaning things, hygiene, solids, liquids and gases. What is inside a bubble? What are the differences between washing-up liquid and water?

- Carry out a survey of the food in your kitchen.

- Food stuffs can be fresh or preserved in some way. Which foods are consumed fresh and which are preserved? How have they been preserved? Make a note of where different types of food are stored and why. Why doesn't food keep indefinitely? Talk about microbes and how they can make things decay.

- Discuss alternative ways of keeping food fresh without a refrigerator, e.g. on a camping holiday or on a mountain climbing expedition.
  Talk to grandparents about how they kept food fresh without a refrigerator.

How do you make so many bubbles?

Mealtimes...

Mealtimes give the opportunity to talk about food and diet. This is part of the Programme of Study for **Sc 2 Life Processes and Living Things**.

- Have a competition at mealtimes or when preparing a meal. Describe the conditions needed for an item of food to grow and ask others to guess the food you are describing.

- Where does the food come from, what is it? If it is a vegetable, which part of the plant is it?

- Look at a variety of fruits and nuts. Cut them up and look inside. What do you notice?

- Which foods are produced in the United Kingdom and which come from countries with warmer climates? Why?

- Find out what vitamins there are in different foods by looking at the packing and labels. What do different vitamins do?

- Make a list of which kind of meat comes from which animal.

- What are the raw materials the food is made from?

What part of me can you eat?

ACTIVITIES   Mealtimes...

- A baby, a teenager and an 80-year-old need different diets to stay healthy. Look at books on health and nutrition to find out which foods each needs to stay healthy.

- Plan a lunch menu for an active 15-year-old boy and one for a woman of 83 who is in average health for her age.

- Prepare and serve a balanced meal for a teenager or an elderly member of your family.

- Where does food go when we eat it?

- Why do we need to eat?

- What do we mean by a healthy balanced diet?

- Make a survey of which foodstuffs contain sugar or salt.

- Which food contains most sugar or salt?

- Talk about the problems connected with eating too much sugary food.

Why are we good for you to eat?

In the Bathroom...

- Some substances are helpful and some are harmful. Drugs can be used beneficially or they can be abused and will harm us. Remember, drug misuse may involve alcohol or smoking.

- Looking in the bathroom cabinet can lead to discussions about drugs as medicine and their safe use. In turn this could lead onto the delicate issues of drug abuse.

- Some people use natural, rather than chemical, remedies to cure ailments and illnesses. Find out about alternative medicines and their uses.

- Visit your dentist. Collect leaflets and posters about looking after your teeth.

- Why is cleaning teeth important? Discuss the importance of dental hygiene and the part bacteria play in decay. What are teeth for? What do they do? Are they all the same? Why not?

- When a tooth falls out will it be replaced?

- Why do we need to wash? Talk about the need for personal cleanliness and hygiene.

- How is soap made?

In the Bathroom...

- Looking in the mirror can lead to discussion about reflections, light and how it travels. Look for mirrors in and around your home.

- How do we actually see? Is our reflection the same as us or is it different?
  What other surfaces reflect light?
  How many different mirrors are in your bathroom?
  Describe how a shaving mirror works.

- Which things float in the bath, and which sink? Why do some things float and others not?

- Can you make a 'floater' sink or a 'sinker' float? How can you do this?

- Why does condensation form on the mirror when you have a shower or a bath?

In the Bathroom...

- What is temperature? How is it measured?
  When is the bath too hot? When is it too cold?
  Talk about the differences between babies and
  adults.

- Talk about body temperatures and what happens
  to temperature when we are sick. Discuss the
  differences between humans who maintain a
  constant body temperature and reptiles which
  regulate their body temperature by exposure to
  the Sun.

- Why does the level of the bath water go up
  when we get in it? Discuss how displacement of
  water can be used to find out the body's or an
  object's volume. Go to the library and find out
  about Archimedes.

- Why do things feel lighter in water?

- Why are bathroom lights usually operated by
  string pulls? Safety issues about electricity can
  be raised along with the idea of which materials
  allow electricity to pass through them and which
  do not (conductors and insulators). How many
  different types of switch are there in your home?
  Talk about how they operate, their differences
  and the reasons for this.

- How do non-slip bath mats work?

In the Garden...

- Visit a park or look in your garden at the variety of plants. Categorise the different plants into:
  – trees, flowers, shrubs;
  – annuals, perrenials

- Plants grow from seeds. What are seeds? How many can you identify in the park or garden? How are they different?

- Discuss the different methods of seed dispersal, e.g. winged 'helicopter' seeds from a sycamore tree. How do seeds start to grow? What are the best conditions for germination?

- Plant some seeds of your own and chart their growth. Note the conditions that lead to healthy growth.

- Make drawings at different stages and keep a diary.

- Why is light important?

- Investigate areas of the garden. How do they differ, e.g. the amount of shade, moisture, different soils?

- How do these differences affect the plants that grow there?

In the Garden...

- Carry out some experiments to find out why water is important for plants.

- How do plants get their food? Discuss your ideas, then look in books for more information.

- Set up an experiment using food colouring to show how plant food travels from the root to the rest of the plant.

- Find out how sunlight is involved in making food for plants.

- Discuss the use of fertilisers and the problems they can cause. Find out about organic food.

- Why is fertiliser used?

- What parts do plants have?
  What are the functions of the parts?
  Root, stem, leaf and flower.

- Collect pictures of plants, or draw them and make a scrapbook. Sort plants into groups using external characteristics.

- Keep a record of wild flowers seen on walks. Note where they were growing (open field, roadside, hedgerow etc.) and identify them using books. Do not pick the flowers.
  Are all the flowers the same? Look at the parts. What does each part do?

In the Garden...

- A garden also provides a home for many creatures, both large and small. Try to encourage care for the environment. Encourage wildlife into your garden by digging a pond or by putting up bird feeders or bird boxes.

- Where do the creatures live? What do they feed on? Where will you find worms, woodlice, bees, snails, spiders, tadpoles, frogs, birds, hedgehogs etc.?

- Set up some simple homes for creatures (vivaria) so they can be studied more closely. A wormery, for example, can be made from a clear plastic box and some earth.

- How can you tell a living thing from something that is not living?

In the Garden...

- Look at the creatures and plants in your garden. Notice their surroundings (habitat). How are the creatures and plants suited to these surroundings?

- What is a food chain? Can you identify some food chains working in the garden? Make drawings to show the different food chains.

- Sort creatures you find in the garden into groups by their external characteristics, such as the number of legs. Use a chart to show the groups you have made.

- Creatures and plants create waste material. What happens to the waste material in a wild garden? Discuss what happens to the waste material in a cultivated garden.

- How is waste recycled? What happens to grass clippings and leaves on a compost heap?

- Where does soil come from?

- What sorts of soil can you have in a garden?

- What makes a good or a poor soil?

- Investigate different soils. Mix some soil in a jar of water and talk about the different layers created when it settles.

In the Garden...

- When you sunbathe, why do you sometimes have to move to stay in the Sun? Talk about the dangers of spending too long in the Sun and the need for sunscreens.

- Record the position of the Sun at different times of the day. Never look directly at the Sun.

- Why does the Sun appear to move?

- Where is the sunniest spot? Which direction does it face?

- Find out about sunrise and sunset, and the 'land of the midnight sun'.

- Study a shadow created by a tree or a post placed in the ground. Measure the change in length in intervals during the day. Does the shadow change in length and direction? Why? Make a chart of your findings.

- How does a sundial work?

In the Garden...

- Investigate different methods of drying clothes. Why does washing hung on a line dry more quickly than washing left in a basket?

- Some materials hold water for longer than others. Why is this? Which materials dry quickly?

- What are the best conditions for drying clothes? Why?

- Look at the ground after it has rained. Where has most of the rainfall gone? If there are puddles, why have they not drained away into the ground? Mark the edge of a puddle at intervals. How long does it take for it to disappear? Where does it go?

- What happens to plants if we have a long, dry summer?

- Why do we sometimes have a hosepipe ban?

Down the Street...

Street and road observations are a very good starting point for thinking about **Physical Processes**.

- Make a study of traffic in a busy street. How many different types of vehicle can you see? How are they powered? What fuel do they use?

- Find out about the different types of fuel used to power vehicles: leaded and unleaded petrol, diesel, gas and electricity. Which is most common? Which is 'cleanest'? Which is most efficient?

- Discuss how vehicles move, speed up, slow down and change direction. What forces are involved in these actions?

Down the Street...

- When you are out shopping or on a car journey, look at the different materials used in buildings and objects.

- Discuss the choices of materials for different purposes, e.g. glass for windows, rubber for tyres. How are these materials made? What are the main components of glass?

- Look at road and pavement surfaces. Can you find any non-slip pavements? How do they work? What are raised studs in the pavement approaching a zebra crossing for? How do they work? What other surfaces do you notice? What is their purpose?

- Look for wheeled machines pushed or pulled by hand, such as trolleys, push chairs, prams and suitcases. What forces are involved in moving these objects?

- Study the sequences involved in traffic lights changing. How do they work?

Down the Street...

- Look for different light sources. How many can you find and how are they generated?

- How are lights dimmed or increased in brightness?

- If you are out at night, when, where and why do you see shadows?
  How does your shadow change as you walk towards and then away from a street lamp?
  Are all the shadows the same? What causes them?

- Why do objects shake when heavy vehicles pass by?
  How do vibrations travel?
  Look for evidence of environmental damage caused by traffic vibrations.

Down the Street...

- Find out about sound – how it travels and is heard; how its intensity is measured.

- Why does the sound of a siren change as it rushes past you? Look it up! It's called the Doppler Effect.

- How are sounds made louder or quieter? How many different sounds can you hear? How do the sounds travel?

On your Bike...

- Riding a bicycle and its maintenance is an excellent source of many ideas about forces and their effects (pushes and pulls, friction, air resistance, springs), light (seeing and being seen, lamps and reflectors), electricity (simple circuits, switches) and sound (bells and horns). For example, how do your brakes work to make you slow down or stop?

- A bicycle and its equipment provide good examples of materials and their properties (tyres, reflective clothing, weatherproof clothing, safety helmets, lightweight frames, brake blocks). For example, how can you make sure you are seen at night?

- Why is it easier to cycle downhill than uphill? What forces are at work?

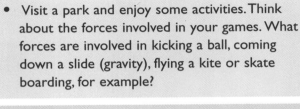

ACTIVITIES In the Park...

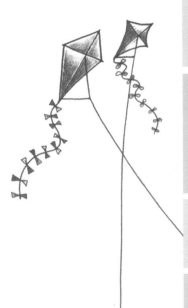

- Visit a park and enjoy some activities. Think about the forces involved in your games. What forces are involved in kicking a ball, coming down a slide (gravity), flying a kite or skate boarding, for example?

- Watch people move, walk, hop, run and jump. What does the skeleton do and how are muscles involved in the movement of our bodies? Find out how many bones make up the human skeleton. Can you name the main bones of the body?

- Measure your pulse rate while resting. Now run or skip for 10 minutes. Measure your pulse rate again. What happens? Why?

- Use library books to find out how the blood is moved around our bodies and how our 'energy' is created.

In the Park...

- How do we breathe and why does our breathing rate increase with exercise?

- What is the function of the heart and lungs?

- How can we make sure that we keep fit?
Plan a schedule of activity for personal fitness.

ACTIVITIES

Up in the Sky...

Use books to investigate these questions:

- 'What goes up must come down.' Is this always true?

- What parts of a bird or plane help it stay in the sky?

- What propels a rocket towards the Moon?

- How do parachutes work? (Air resistance)

- How can we tell that the Earth spins?

- Devise some experiments of your own to test methods of slowing an object's speed of fall to the ground.

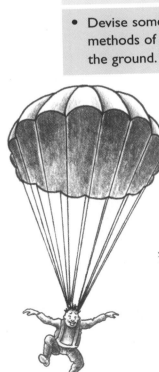

Up in the Sky...

- Observe the night sky, the Moon and stars. What are the phases of the Moon? How long do they last? Make a record.

- Can we see any planets? Which ones?

- Make a scrapbook of all you find out about the solar system.

- How far away are the stars?

- What is a rainbow? When can you see one? How is it formed?

- Can you see any other 'rainbows' anywhere other than in the sky?

- Where does rain come from and where does it go? (The water cycle)

At the Doctor's...

- A visit to the doctor's or hospital is a good opportunity to discuss any health-related issues.

- How can we keep a healthy heart?

- What are bones and how are they mended?

- How do muscles get 'pulled' or strained?

- What are joints and how do they work?

- Look at the posters on the wall.
  Design posters about smoking or alcohol abuse.

- Talk to your family about the illnesses and injuries that they have had. Could they have been prevented? How did they get well or fit again?

Can I stay fit by running?

At the Doctor's...

- Use reference books to research the link between microbes and disease.

- How can some common diseases be prevented or cured?

- Look at old photographs of the family and talk about how people change as they get older.

- Talk about where babies come from.

- How do our bodies change as we get older, e.g. puberty, old age (the human life cycle).

- Talk to a grandparent about the illnesses that were suffered when they were young. Which illnesses are still around today?

- Talk to a grandparent about how medical services have changed.

- Find out about scientists who have helped to improve medical care and medicine.

This is where it all starts.

Relaxing at Home...

- Talk about electrical safety in the home.

- Try to find ways of stopping sound from travelling (insulation materials).

- How far can sound travel? For example, can you hear a penny drop? How far away do you get before you can't hear it drop?

- Play or listen to musical instruments.
  How do instruments make their different sounds?

- How can you change the pitch to play higher or lower?

- How can you change the volume to play louder or softer?

- Try making a musical instrument from everyday objects.

- How many different examples of uses for electricity can you find? (light, heat, sound, movement...) Make a list or a collage using pictures cut out from magazines.

- Look around the home for different materials, e.g. wood, plastic and metal. Make a list of items that are made from these materials because of their properties (hard, waterproof, heat insulator etc.).

Relaxing at Home...

- Caring for pets can be the starting point for the study of living things. What do they need for a healthy life?

- Make a booklet about caring for a pet. Study your pet and use books for information. Make a schedule for looking after the pet. This should involve:
    - feeding
    - cleaning
    - exercise
    - care and attention, such as grooming

- How can we keep ourselves warm or cool? How can we keep the house warm?

- Look at fast food packaging. How does it keep the food warm? How does a food cooler work?

- What do all living things do? What life processes do they show?

- What do living things need in order to survive?

- What is their life cycle?

- What similarities and differences are there between the needs of the people and the animals in your home?

GLOSSARY

This explains some of the scientific words used in the Homework Activity Book.

adapted
Having certain characteristics which fit or suit a plant or an animal to its habitat, so helping it to survive.

air resistance
A force exerted by the air against a moving object. A form of friction.

anther
The part of a flower which produces pollen. It is at the top of the stamen.

artery
Blood vessels that carry blood away from the heart.

attract
Unlike poles of a magnet attract each other. They pull towards each other.

Celsius
Temperature is measured in degrees Celsius (^oC).

characteristic
Something peculiar or particular about an object or living thing.

circuit
A system of batteries, wires and components through which electricity can pass.

condense
To change from a gas to a liquid, for example, water vapour to water. The opposite of evaporate.

conductor
A material through which electricity can pass easily is an electrical conductor. A material through which heat can pass easily is a thermal conductor.

consumer
Part of a food chain, an animal that eats something else.

dispersal
The way in which seeds travel away from the parent plant.

dissolve
A solid 'dissolves' in a liquid to form a solution.

evaporate
To change from liquid to a gas, for example water to water vapour. The opposite of condensation.

environment
A plant's or animal's surroundings. An interrelationship of plants and animals in a particular area.

filter
A fine 'sieve' often made of paper, used to separate soluble from insoluble solids.

food chain
A way to describe feeding relationships. What is eaten by what and so on…

force
A push, a pull or combination of these, such as a twist. Force is measured using a forcemeter or newtonmeter.

freeze
To change from a liquid to a solid, for example water to ice. The opposite of melt.

friction
A force that acts against movement.
The result of two surfaces rubbing
together or moving past each other. Air
resistance is a form of friction.

fuel
A material burned to release energy.

germination
The point at which a seed starts to
grow into a seedling.

gravity
The force exerted by the Earth
pulling towards its centre.

habitat
The immediate surroundings of a
plant or animal to which it must be
adapted in order to survive.

insulator
A material through which electricity
cannot pass easily is an electrical
insulator.
A material through which heat cannot
pass easily is a thermal insulator.

key
A method of identifying animals and
plants by their chaaracteristics.

magnet
Usually a piece of iron or steel which
exerts a magnetic force.

magnetic
Materials that are attracted to a magnet.

mass
The amount of 'stuff' or matter in a
material. Mass is measured in kilograms.

melt
To change from a solid into a liquid,
for example ice to water.
The opposite of freeze.

microbe
A tiny single-celled organism that can
cause decay and disease, for example
a bacteria.

mixture
When two or more different
materials or substances are put
together. Mixtures can usually be
'unmixed'.

newton
The unit of measurement of force (N).

opaque
Materials that light will not pass
through. It will make a shadow.

orbit
The track taken by a planet as it
travels round the Sun. The track
taken by the moon as it travels
round the Earth.

petal
The part of a flower which provides
a landing place for insects.
The petal is often brightly coloured
to attract them.

pitch
The level of a musical note, 'high' or
'low'.

pole
The opposite ends or sides of a
magnet, north and south.

pollen
The male reproductive material of
a flowering plant which fertilises
the ovary or egg.

predator
A creature that feeds on other
creatures.

prey
A creature that is eaten by another creature.

producer
A green plant which converts the Sun's energy into food.
There is usually a producer at the start of every food chain.

property
A characteristic of an object or material.

reflection
An image formed in a mirror or other shiny surface when light is 'bounced back' to the eye.

repel
The like poles of a magnet repel each other. They push each other away.

shadow
Formed when an object made from an opaque material 'blocks' the path of light.

sieve
A mesh of wire or similar material which is used to grade or sort material with different sized particles.

stamen
The male part of a flowering plant.

stigma
The sticky tip of the female part of a flowering plant to which pollen will stick.

switch
A device for turning a circuit on or off.

temperature
The measurement of hot or cold. Measured with a thermometer.

transparent
Material that light will pass through, material that you can see through.

translucent
Material that light will pass through, but not enough to see through.

upthrust
A force which opposes gravity. Gravity pulls down on objects trying to make them 'sink' and upthrust pushes up. If the two forces become equal than the object will 'float'.

vibration
The source of a sound.

weight
The effect of gravity on mass. Gravity pulls down on objects giving them weight. Weight should properly be measured in newtons because it is a force.